Time to try.... the LOW FODMAP DIET

CookNation

Time to try...the LOW FODMAP DIET

Complete plan for managing symptoms of IBS, Crohn's disease, coeliac disease and other digestive disorders

ISBN 978-1-912511-05-1

Cover image under license from Shutterstock

Disclaimer

This book is designed to provide information on the popular Low FODMAP Diet. Some recipes may contain nuts or traces of nuts. Those suffering from any allergies associated with nuts should avoid any recipes containing nuts or nut based oils.
This information is provided and sold with the knowledge that the publisher and author do not offer any legal or other professional advice.
In the case of a need for any such expertise consult with the appropriate professional.
This book does not contain all information available on the subject, and other sources of recipes are available.
Every effort has been made to make this book as accurate as possible. However, there may be typographical and or content errors. Therefore, this book should serve only as a general guide and not as the ultimate source of subject information.
This book contains information that might be dated and is intended only to educate and entertain.
The author and publisher shall have no liability or responsibility to any person or entity regarding any loss or damage incurred, or alleged to have incurred, directly or indirectly, by the information contained in this book.

CONTENTS

INTRODUCTION

Ease Your Tummy Troubles and Feel Better: Try the Low FODMAP Diet for Beginners

Many people experience bloating, gas or constipation from time to time and most would attribute that to the big meal they ate the night before or an indulgent dessert they've eaten. However some people experience these types of symptoms time and time again– so, what if you're suffering from these symptoms on a regular basis?

Some people suffer from stomach-related symptoms for months or even years before considering a particular food or food group could be to blame and that by cutting out these foods they would feel better and have less tummy trouble.

The low FODMAP diet is now widely accepted as a credible option for helping people manage stomach pain or discomfort caused by diet.

What is FODMAP and How Did it Start? A Brief History

FODMAP foods are those that are made up of certain carbohydrates and molecules, which may be difficult for people with sensitive stomachs to digest. The name itself stands for: Fermentable Oligosaccharides, Disaccharides, Monosaccharides and Polyols' – the official names of the elements found naturally in some foods. These foods have been divided into those that contain a high level of these elements, and those that are not. High FODMAP foods are then restricted or removed from the diet, in order to find out which are causing a sufferer discomfort.

The diet came about in the early 1990s in Australia when patients with stomach problems were placed on a diet which removed foods containing fructose. By cutting out or cutting down on some fructose-based foods, many of those patients had great results, finding that their symptoms improved.

After this success, the diet then evolved to include some other foods that contain other molecular make-up, such as carbohydrates, thought to bring on certain symptoms. The diet has since had year-on-year success - to the point where it is now suggested by dieticians and has become a commonplace diet for people to use. People with sensitive stomachs and IBS symptoms, such as nausea, bloating, constipation and stomach cramps, have had improved symptoms after adjusting their diets in this way.

How to get started

For anyone considering starting any kind of diet, it is strongly advised that they consult with their doctor first. A doctor will be able to carry out any tests needed to find a diagnosis for your stomach symptoms and make professional recommendations, letting you know if it is safe to go onto this diet. You can then find a dietician or nutritionist to advise you on how to approach the diet and suggest appropriate meals, including portion sizes, to follow.

Why you would choose a low FODMAP diet - how it works

A low FODMAP diet is ideal for people who suffer regular symptoms of IBS, such as constipation, nausea, acid reflux and diarrhoea. The diet works as a two-step approach. The first step involves the 'elimination' stage, which involves taking certain high FODMAP foods out of your diet to clear your body of them and the carbohydrates they contain.

The second step is called the 'reintroduction' stage, which involves introducing the high FODMAP foods back into your diet, one at a time, and done this way, you will be able to work out which foods are causing your symptoms. It is recommended that this stage of the diet is only tried for a matter of weeks, as cutting out certain foods from your diet for longer may be unhealthy.

The food included in the diet can be prepared in meals that do not take anymore time than you would usually take to cook.

Unlike many other diets that ban chocolate and sugary snacks, this diet still allows for many foods not traditionally included in a 'normal' diet - these include chocolate and some snacks. They can occasionally be consumed in small amounts.

Foods Considered as High FODMAP

The FODMAP diet outlines a wide range of food that cannot be eaten for the duration of the diet, and those that cannot. Although they are deemed healthy, some of the foods below are considered to have a high FODMAP and may surprise you:

- Some fruits, including apples, pears, peaches, plums and nectarines
- Vegetables, including mushrooms, garlic, onions, asparagus and cauliflower
- Milk – the diet often recommends using lactose-free milk
- Wheat-based foods
- Lentils
- Cashews
- Honey

Foods Classed as Low FODMAP

For your meal planner, put together foods classed as 'low FODMAP', which you are able to eat, will include:

- Fruit including avocados, bananas, limes, pineapple, grapes and strawberries
- Vegetables include cucumber, olives, broccoli, capsicum, carrots, olives, spinach, tomatoes
- Some milk products, such as butter, Brie, parmesan, butter, cheddar, mozzarella and some yoghurts
- Gluten-free bread/pasta/biscuits etc, rice, and quinoa
- A range of other foods, including garlic-infused olive oil, peanut butter, tea, fish, tofu and eggs

Why It's Healthy

The foods that a dieter can eat are still very varied and contain a range from each food group, including fruit, vegetables, protein, nuts and dairy products. There is also some dairy and all of the milk options are either lactose-free or offer alternative forms, such as almond or soy milk. There are many low FODMAP options available that contain a wide range of vitamins ad balanced nutritional benefits.

The diet includes plenty of fruit and veg but like many diets, still contains some restrictions on what you can have and isn't recommended on a long-term basis. However, that's why it's important to have your dietician on board, to help ensure that these foods are well-balanced in the diet, as well as advising on the appropriate portions.

Why a low FODMAP diet will help you

The strategic approach to this diet helps to rule out the foods causing symptoms, and those that are not. With the knowledge of the 'trigger' foods, it is high likely that you'll find out the foods you are sensitive to. Dieters can then be supported to continue leaving out the food, whilst maintaining a healthy diet.

Once you have figured out the culprit foods for you, you can then choose not to eat these foods - or eat them in moderation - so that you suffer less symptoms, or prevent them.

The diet has seen great success with many people, who have been able to find out which foods trigger their symptoms. By cutting these foods out of their diets, they have experienced less symptoms - or none at all.

About CookNation

CookNation is the leading publisher of innovative and practical recipe books for the modern, health conscious cook.

CookNation titles bring together delicious, easy and practical recipes with their unique no-nonsense approach - making cooking for diets and healthy eating fast, simple and fun.

With a range of #1 best-selling titles - from the innovative 'Skinny' calorie-counted series, to the 5:2 Diet Recipes collection - CookNation recipe books prove that 'Diet' can still mean 'Delicious'!

Visit **www.bellmackenzie.com** to browse the full catalogue.

CookNation

15

Low FODMAP

BREAKFASTS

Time to try....

the LOW FODMAP DIET

SERVES 6

Muesli

Low FODMAP Diet

Ingredients

- 250g/9oz gluten-free cornflakes, lightly crushed
- 6 tbsp desiccated coconut
- 4 tbsp pumpkin seeds
- 40g/1½oz quinoa puffs
- 60g/2½oz brown sugar
- 6 tbsp olive oil
- 25g/1oz banana chips

Method

1 Preheat the oven to 150C/300F/Gas.2 Line a baking tray with parchment.

2 In a bowl mix together the cornflakes, shredded coconut, pumpkin seeds, quinoa puffs and brown sugar. Stir in the oil until everything is evenly coated.

3 Tip the mixture out onto the lined baking tray and spread evenly. Toast in the oven for around 20 minutes, stirring once, until the muesli is a light golden brown. Remove from the oven and leave to cool.

4 When the muesli is cooled, stir in the banana chips. Store in an airtight container for up to two weeks.

Chefs Note....

Enjoy with low FodMap milk – e.g. soy, oat, macadamia, etc. - or with fruit.

Eggs Florentine

SERVES 4

Low FODMAP Diet

Ingredients

- 60ml/¼ cup white wine vinegar
- 6 whole black peppercorns
- 2 egg yolks
- 200g/7oz unsalted butter, melted
- Salt & pepper
- 2 tsp lemon juice
- 8 rashers bacon
- 25g/1oz butter
- 2 handfuls spinach leaves
- Dash white vinegar
- 4 fresh eggs, room temperature
- 4 slices gluten-free bread, toasted

Method

1 In a saucepan, heat the vinegar and peppercorns to a simmer, and cook uncovered, for around 5 minutes, until the mixture reduces to about 2 tsp. Strain the liquid through a fine sieve into a heatproof bowl.

2 Place the bowl over a pan of boiling water, and whisk in the eggs. Still whisking, slowly pour in the melted butter and continue to whisk until the mixture is thick and creamy.

3 Remove the bowl from the heat. Season to taste with salt and pepper and lemon juice. Cover and set aside.

4 In a frying pan, fry the bacon until crispy, then remove it to a plate. Melt the butter in the same pan, then add the spinach and cook, stirring, for about 4 minutes until the spinach wilts. Season with salt and pepper.

5 Add a dash of vinegar to a pan of water and bring to the boil, then lower the heat to a simmer. Stir the water to create a whirlpool and crack in the eggs to poach, one at a time. Cook the eggs for 2-4 minutes, according to whether you prefer them soft or harder. Transfer them to a plate using a slotted spoon and cover to keep warm.

6 Arrange the toast on 4 serving plates with the spinach and bacon over each slice. Place the poached eggs on top and drizzle with the hollandaise sauce. Season and serve at once.

SERVES 6

Coconut Granola with Vanilla Cream

Low FODMAP Diet

Ingredients

- 100g/3½oz oat flour
- 100g/3½oz desiccated coconut
- 3 tbsp coconut oil, melted, + some for greasing
- 2 tbsp maple syrup
- Pinch sea salt
- 400ml/14floz tin full-fat coconut milk, refrigerated overnight
- 1 tsp vanilla extract

Method

1 Preheat the oven to 180C/350F/Gas4.

2 In a bowl, mix together the oat flour, desiccated coconut, coconut oil, and maple syrup.

3 Grease a small baking tray with coconut oil and press the mixture into the bottom of it. Bake in the oven for about 15 minutes until crisp, then set aside to cool.

4 Meanwhile, spoon off the cream which has formed at the top of your tin of coconut milk and drop it into a bowl. Using an electric mixer, whisk it well until it's fluffy and forms soft peaks. Stir in the vanilla.

5 When the granola is cool, break it into chunks and divide it between 6 bowls. Serve with the vanilla cream.

Chefs Note....
Feel free to add dark chocolate or fresh low FodMap fruit.

SERVES 1

Breakfast Wrap

Low FODMAP Diet

Ingredients

- Cooking spray
- 2 eggs
- 1 tsp fresh chives, finely chopped
- 1 small gluten-free wrap
- 1 handful rocket
- ½ tomato, sliced
- 25g/1oz avocado, sliced

Method

1 Lightly spray a small frying pan with oil, and heat.

2 In a bowl, beat the eggs with the chives. Pour the eggs into the pan and cook for about 2 minutes or until almost set, then turn over and cook for another 30 seconds or so.

3 Meanwhile, put the wrap on a plate and heat it in the microwave for 10 seconds.

4 Place the egg on top of the wrap. Add the rocket, tomato and avocado. Fold up the wrap, and enjoy.

Chefs Note....

Make sure your wrap is a gluten free variety that is also free of high FodMap ingredients such as inulin.

Pancakes

MAKES 16 PANCAKES

Low FODMAP Diet

Ingredients

- 200g/7oz gluten free flour, sifted
- 2 tsp xanthan gum
- 2 tbsp brown sugar
- 1 tbsp baking powder
- 1 tsp salt
- 1 tsp ground cinnamon
- ¼ tsp ground nutmeg
- ¼ tsp ground ginger
- 500ml/2 cups lactose free milk
- 425g/15oz tinned pumpkin puree
- 2 eggs
- 2 tbsp vegetable oil

Method

1 In a bowl mix together the flour, xanthan gum, sugar, baking powder, salt, cinnamon, nutmeg, and ginger.

2 In a smaller bowl whisk the milk, pumpkin puree, eggs, and oil.

3 Pour the pumpkin mixture into the flour and stir to make a batter. Set aside to rest for 5 minutes.

4 Heat a frying pan or griddle and lightly grease. Allow about 60ml/¼ cup batter for each pancake. Pour them one at a time onto pan or griddle and cook for a couple of minutes on each side until the pancakes are golden brown.

5 Serve warm with your favourite topping.

Chefs Note....

Try with blueberries, raspberries, mandarin oranges or maple syrup.

SERVES 2

Quinoa Porridge

Low FODMAP Diet

Ingredients

- 100g/3½oz quinoa, rinsed
- 1 tsp sunflower oil
- 250ml/1 cup water
- 250ml/1 cup soy milk
- ¼ tsp ground cinnamon
- 4 tsp maple syrup

Method

1 Tip the quinoa into a pan with a little sunflower oil. Cook for a couple of minutes until the water has evaporated and the quinoa is lightly toasted.

2 Pour in the water and bring to the boil. Reduce the heat, cover and cook for about 15 minutes until the quinoa is fluffy. Drain.

3 Add the soy milk, cinnamon, and maple syrup. Simmer the porridge for about 5 minutes until hot right through.

4 Serve with your favourite low FodMap fruit, e.g. raspberries, blueberries etc.

Chefs Note....
Use any low FodMap milk you prefer instead of soy, e.g. oat, almond, hemp or coconut.

SERVES 4

Baked Ham and Eggs with Toast

Low FODMAP Diet

Ingredients

- 8 slices ham
- 150g/5oz baby spinach
- 2 tbsp Parmesan cheese, grated
- 4 eggs
- 4 slices gluten free bread, toasted

Method

1 Preheat the oven to 180C/350F/Gas4.

2 Lightly grease four small ovenproof dishes. Line each with 2 slices of ham to cover the bases and sides.

3 Wilt the spinach by microwaving it for 1-1½ minutes. Tip the spinach into a sieve and press down with the back of a spoon to squeeze out excess water.

4 Distribute the spinach between the 4 dishes, then scatter each with the Parmesan.

5 Crack an egg into each dish and season them with salt and pepper. Bake in the oven for 18-20 minutes or until the egg white is set.

6 Take them out of the oven, leave to stand for 2 minutes, then serve with the toast.

Chefs Note....

Makes a special breakfast or a lovely light lunch or supper.

SERVES 8

Tangerine and Banana Granola

Low FODMAP Diet

Ingredients

- 200g/7oz oatmeal
- 2 tbsp uncooked quinoa
- 2 tbsp flax seeds
- 3 tbsp pumpkin seeds
- 100g/3½oz pecan nuts
- 60g/2½oz banana chips
- Zest of 2 tangerines
- 1 tsp salt
- ½ tsp cinnamon
- 60ml/¼ cup maple syrup
- 2 tbsp brown sugar
- 2 tbsp coconut oil, melted

Method

1 Preheat the oven to 150C/300F/Gas2. Line a large baking tray with parchment.

2 In a large bowl, mix together the oats, quinoa, flax seeds, pumpkin seeds, pecans, banana chips, tangerine zest, salt and cinnamon.

3 Stir in the maple syrup, sugar and oil until all the dry ingredients are well coated.

4 Tip the mixture out onto the baking tray and spread it evenly.

5 Bake in the oven for 20-30 minutes, stirring every ten minutes or so, until golden brown.

6 Allow the granola to cool completely before serving with low FodMap yoghurt or milk.

Chefs Note....

Be careful not to use more than 1/8 of it in one sitting, since this might take you over your oat allowance.

SERVES 1

Spiced Coffee Oats

Low FODMAP Diet

Ingredients

- 250ml/1 cup almond milk
- 25g/1oz rolled oats
- 1 tsp instant coffee granules
- Pinch ground cinnamon
- 2 tsp maple syrup
- 15g/½oz walnuts, chopped
- 25g/1oz fresh blueberries

Method

1 Pour the milk into a pan. Add the oats, coffee, cinnamon and maple syrup, and heat until the milk starts to simmer.

2 Lower the heat and cook gently, stirring occasionally, for about 5 minutes or until the mixture is the consistency you prefer.

3 Tip the mixture out into a bowl and scatter on the walnuts and blueberries.

4 Eat and enjoy.

Chefs Note....
Use frozen blueberries if you prefer, and substitute any low FodMap milk you prefer in place of the almond milk.

SERVES 1

Tropical Pancakes

Low FODMAP Diet

Ingredients

- 2 eggs
- 1 un-ripened banana, peeled & mashed
- 25g/1oz coconut flour
- Pinch salt
- 1 tbsp coconut oil

Method

1 In a bowl, whisk together the eggs, mashed banana, coconut flour and salt.

2 Heat the coconut oil in a large frying pan. Pour in the mixture in 2 or 3 dollops, and fry for about 2 minutes on each side, until golden brown.

3 Serve with a handful of berries and a dollop of lactose free yoghurt.

Chefs Note....
Coconut flour is naturally sweet so makes delicious pancakes.

SERVES 1

Chilled Chocolate and Banana Oats

Low FODMAP Diet

Ingredients

- 25g/1oz oats
- 2 tbsp almond milk
- 1 tsp unsweetened cocoa powder
- ½ un-ripened banana, mashed
- 2 tbsp lactose-free yogurt
- Dash vanilla extract
- 2 tsp maple syrup
- 1/2 tsp ground cinnamon
- 25g/1oz dark chocolate, broken into chunks, to garnish
- A few fresh banana slices, to garnish

Method

1 In a medium bowl, stir together the oats and the almond milk. Then stir in the cocoa, banana, yogurt, vanilla, maple syrup, and cinnamon.

2 Tip the mixture into an airtight container and chill in the fridge overnight.

3 In the morning, top with the chocolate chunks and banana slices and serve.

Chefs Note....

A luxurious low FodMap breakfast sure to be popular with both adults and children.

SERVES 1

Eggs in Red Pepper

Low FODMAP Diet

Ingredients

- Cooking spray
- 1 red pepper, de-seeded and sliced into 1½cm rings
- 2 eggs
- 2 tsp chives, finely chopped
- Handful rocket
- 1 slice gluten-free bread, toasted

Method

1. Heat a frying pan and spray it lightly with oil.
2. Add the two widest pepper rings to the pan and then scatter half the chives inside them.
3. Crack an egg into each ring and sprinkle the remaining chives on top. Fry the eggs to the consistency you like.
4. Serve the rings on a bed of rocket with a slice of toast on the side. Season with salt and pepper, and eat!

Chefs Note....

If you prefer, substitute a chopped fresh herb, such as parsley or basil, for the chives.

SERVES 4

Fruit with Yogurt and Syrup

Low FODMAP Diet

Ingredients

- 100g/3½oz caster sugar
- 250g/9oz strawberries, hulled & halved
- 150g/5oz blueberries
- 125g/4oz raspberries
- 250g/8oz Greek style yoghurt

Method

1 Heat the sugar in a pan over low heat, stirring occasionally until the sugar dissolves and turns golden brown.

2 Meanwhile, mix the berries together in a serving bowl. Pour the yoghurt over the berries, then drizzle the syrup over the top.

3 Serve and enjoy.

Chefs Note....

If you're lactose intolerant, use lactose free yogurt instead, and you can double the quantity.

SERVES 1

Coconut Porridge with Kiwi Fruit

Low FODMAP Diet

Ingredients

- 250ml/1 cup almond milk
- 25g/1oz porridge oats
- 1 tbsp desiccated coconut
- 1 tsp sugar
- ¼ tsp vanilla extract
- 1 kiwi fruit, peeled & sliced
- 2 tbsp pumpkin seeds

Method

1 Pour the milk into a pan. Stir in the oats, coconut, sugar and vanilla.

2 Heat until the mixture begins to simmer, then lower the heat and cook for about 5 minutes, stirring occasionally, until the porridge reaches the consistency you like.

3 Tip it out into a bowl and arrange the kiwi fruit on top. Scatter on the pumpkin seeds and serve.

Chefs Note....

Kiwi fruits are both high in fibre and low in FodMaps, so they're a great way to boost your intake of dietary fibre.

MAKES 12 SCONES

Potato Scones

Low FODMAP Diet

Ingredients

- 400g/14oz potatoes, peeled & cooked
- 75g/3oz gluten-free self-raising flour, + extra for rolling
- Pinch salt
- Cooking spray

Method

1 Mash the potatoes in a bowl, then stir in the flour and the salt to make a stiff dough.

2 Divide the dough evenly into three parts. Roll each part out into a circle shape and quarter them until you have 12 scones.

3 Heat your frying pan or griddle and spray lightly with oil. Cook the scones in batches for 3-4 minutes on each side.

4 Serve warm.

Chefs Note....

Cook extra potatoes with dinner the night before and enjoy potato scones for breakfast.

20

Low FODMAP

LUNCHES

Time to try....
the
LOW FODMAP
DIET

Chickpeas on Toast

SERVES 4

Low FODMAP Diet

Ingredients

- 165g/5½oz tinned chickpeas, rinsed & drained
- 225g/8oz passata/sieved tomatoes
- ½ tsp paprika
- ½ tsp Worcestershire sauce
- 4 slices gluten free bread

Method

1 In a pan, mix together the chickpeas, passata, paprika and Worcestershire sauce. Heat gently.

2 Meanwhile, toast the bread.

3 When ready to serve, pour the chickpea mixture over the toast.

Chefs Note....

A fantastic low FodMap substitute for beans on toast! Just be careful to buy passata that has no onion or garlic added.

SERVES 4

Minestrone

Low FODMAP Diet

Ingredients

- 1 tbsp garlic infused olive oil
- 3 rashers middle bacon, chopped
- 75g/3oz leeks, green parts only, finely chopped
- 2 large carrots, peeled & diced
- 1 small potato, peeled & diced
- 1 stalk celery, finely sliced
- Dash olive oil
- 500ml/2 cups of gluten free, low FodMap vegetable stock
- 400g/14oz can chopped tomatoes
- 250ml/1 cup boiling water
- 60g/2½oz spinach leaves, chopped
- 1 courgette, diced
- 200g/7oz tinned chickpeas, drained & rinsed
- 1 tbsp fresh basil, chopped
- 75g/3oz gluten free pasta
- Salt & pepper

Method

1 In a large pan, heat the garlic infused oil, and sauté the bacon, leek, carrot, potato and celery for about 10 minutes until the vegetables begin to soften.

2 Add a dash of plain olive oil and reduce the heat.

3 Pour in the tomatoes, stock and hot water, then stir in the spinach, courgette and chickpeas. Bring to the boil, then reduce the heat and simmer for 10 minutes.

4 Add the pasta and basil to the soup and cook for another 10 minutes or so until the pasta is done.

5 Season with salt and pepper and serve with a sprinkling of Parmesan cheese and a few fresh basil leaves.

Chefs Note....
Making your own vegetable stock is ideal but if you use stock cubes etc, be sure to check the ingredients.

Rice and Tuna Salad

SERVES 4

Low FODMAP Diet

Ingredients

- 450g/1lb brown rice, cooked weight
- 75g/3oz green beans, cooked
- 2 medium tomatoes, diced
- 3 spring onions, green parts only, thinly sliced
- 2 x 160g/5½oz cans tuna in spring water
- 2 lemons, 1 juiced, 1 cut into wedges
- 1 tbsp olive oil

Method

1 In a large bowl, mix together the boiled rice, green beans, tomatoes and spring onions. Drain the tuna and flake it with a fork into chunks. Tip it into the rice and toss gently.

2 In a small bowl whisk together the lemon juice and olive oil. Season well with salt and pepper, then pour it over the rice dish and toss gently to coat everything in the dressing.

3 Serve in bowls, garnished with the lemon wedges.

Chefs Note....
Be careful not to use the white part of the spring onions which is high FodMap.

SERVES 8

Ratatouille

Low FODMAP Diet

Ingredients

- 4 tbsp olive oil
- 1 aubergine, chopped
- Salt & pepper to taste
- 2 courgettes, chopped
- 1 red pepper, deseeded & chopped
- 175g/6oz green beans
- 400g/14oz can chopped tomatoes
- 1 tsp dried oregano
- 40g/1½oz olives, pitted & chopped
- 125g/4oz feta cheese, crumbled
- Chopped fresh basil

Method

1 Heat 2 tbsp oil in a frying pan. Season the aubergine with salt and black pepper, and sauté it in the pan for 8-10 minutes, until it's lightly browned. Tip it into a large bowl.

2 Heat 1 tbsp oil in the same pan, and gently fry the courgette and pepper for 5 minutes. Empty it into the bowl with the aubergine.

3 Heat the remaining oil in the pan. Sauté the green beans for about 3 minutes, then stir in the tomatoes and bring to a simmer. Tip the vegetables in the bowl back into the frying pan and stir in the oregano.

4 Cover, reduce the heat and simmer for 25-30 minutes, stirring occasionally, until the vegetables are very tender. Stir in the olives and adjust the seasoning.

5 Serve scattered with feta and fresh basil.

Chefs Note....

Delicious on its own, or with gluten free pasta, polenta, rice or quinoa.

SERVES 4

Egg with Spicy Vegetables

Low FODMAP Diet

Ingredients

- 1 tbsp garlic infused olive oil
- 1 red pepper, deseeded & cut into strips
- 60g/2½oz spinach leaves, chopped
- 15g/½oz spring onion, green parts only, finely chopped
- 400g/14oz can chopped tomatoes
- 1 tbsp cornflour
- 250ml/1 cup gluten-free, low FodMap chicken stock
- 1 tsp paprika
- 1 tsp ground cumin
- Pinch chilli flakes
- Salt & pepper
- 4 eggs

Method

1. Heat the oil in a large frying pan and sauté the pepper until it softens. Stir in the tomatoes and chicken stock and bring to a simmer.
2. In a small bowl mix the cornflour with a little warm water to make a smooth paste. Pour it into the pepper and tomato mixture, stirring constantly until completely combined.
3. Stir in the spinach and the spring onion and cook for another couple of minutes until the sauce thickens.
4. Stir in the paprika, cumin and chilli flakes. Season to taste and reduce the heat.
5. Being careful to space them evenly, crack the eggs on top of the mixture. Cover and cook for 10-15 minutes, until the eggs are the consistency you prefer.
6. Serve with gluten free bread, and garnished with a little extra spinach if you like.

Chefs Note....

Although garlic itself should be avoided in a low FodMap diet, garlic-infused oil is safe because the FodMaps in garlic are only water soluble and will not contaminate the oil.

SERVES 2

Quinoa and Chickpea Salad

Low FODMAP Diet

Ingredients

- 3 tsp extra virgin olive oil
- 1 tsp of white balsamic vinegar
- 100g/3½oz quinoa, well rinsed & cooked
- 75g/3oz canned chickpeas, well-rinsed & drained
- 60g/2½oz cucumber, chopped
- 2 radishes, finely sliced
- 125g/4oz cherry tomatoes, quartered
- 2 tbsp pumpkin seeds
- 2 handfuls mixed salad leaves, roughly chopped

Method

1 In a small bowl, whisk together the olive oil and balsamic to make a dressing.

2 In a large bowl, mix together the quinoa, chickpeas, cucumber, radishes, tomatoes, pumpkin seeds and salad leaves.

3 Drizzle the dressing over the top and toss everything together until it's evenly coated in the dressing.

4 Serve in 2 bowls.

Chefs Note....
Tinned chickpeas are lower in FodMaps than fresh.

SERVES 4

Carrot and Ginger Soup

Low FODMAP Diet

Ingredients

- 1 tbsp olive oil
- 6 large carrots, peeled & chopped
- 3 medium parsnips, peeled & chopped
- 1 tsp freshly grated ginger
- 1lt/4 cups gluten free, low FodMap vegetable stock
- 4 tbsp coconut milk
- 1 tsp turmeric
- 1 tbsp paprika
- Salt & pepper
- Sunflower seeds, to garnish

Method

1 Heat the oil in a large pan and sauté the carrots, parsnip and ginger for about 8 minutes to soften.

2 Pour in the stock, then stir in the turmeric and paprika and season with salt and pepper.

3 Bring to the boil, then reduce the heat, cover and simmer for about 20 minutes or until the vegetables are soft.

4 Leave the soup to cool for a few minutes, then stir in the coconut milk and blend until smooth.

5 Ladle into bowls and garnish with sunflower seeds and a swirl of coconut milk if you wish.

Chefs Note....
Enjoy with a slice of gluten-free bread.

SERVES 4

Chicken and Grape Salad

Low FODMAP Diet

Ingredients

- 1 bunch watercress
- 1 fennel bulb, grated
- 250g/½lb red seedless grapes, halved
- 300g/11oz chicken breast, cooked & sliced
- 60ml/¼ cup pomegranate dressing

Method

1 In a bowl, mix together the watercress, fennel and grapes. Add the chicken slices and toss gently.

2 Divide the chicken salad among 4 serving plates and drizzle the pomegranate dressing over each.

Chefs Note....

Although pomegranates are high FodMap fruits, most people will tolerate ½ a small one, so the small amounts in a drizzle of dressing should be safe. It tastes delicious! But if you have doubts, try another fruit dressing instead.

SERVES 4

Courgette and Mint Soup

Low FODMAP Diet

Ingredients

- 3 tbsp olive oil
- 1 carrot, peeled & diced
- 1 medium potato, peeled & diced
- 4 courgettes, roughly chopped
- 750ml/3 cups gluten free, low FodMap vegetable stock
- 2 tbsp fresh mint, chopped
- Salt & pepper
- 2 slices gluten free bread, cut into cubes
- 2 tbsp Parmesan cheese, grated
- 2 tbsp lactose free crème fraiche

Method

1 Heat 2 tbsp of the oil in a large pan and sauté the carrot and potato for 5 minutes until they begin to soften. Add the courgettes and cook for a couple of minutes more.

2 Pour in the stock and add the mint. Season with salt and pepper.

3 Bring to the boil, reduce the heat and cook, covered, for about 20 minutes until all the vegetables are soft.

4 Allow to cool for a few minutes, then blend until smooth.

5 Meanwhile, make the croutons by frying the bread cubes in the remaining olive oil until golden brown and crispy. Season with a pinch of salt.

6 Just before serving, stir the Parmesan cheese and crème fraiche into the soup. Ladle the soup into bowls. Scatter the croutons on top and garnish with a sprig of fresh mint.

Chefs Note....

Make your own vegetable stock, or carefully check the ingredients of stock cubes etc.

SERVES 2

Leek and Tomato Frittata

Low FODMAP Diet

Ingredients

- 3 tsp olive oil
- 50g/2oz leek, green parts only, chopped
- Salt & pepper
- 100g/3½oz tomatoes, chopped
- 40g/1½oz capers, rinsed and drained
- 3 egg whites, + 2 yolks
- 1 tsp dried herbes de Provence
- 1 tsp dried thyme
- 50g/2oz goat's cheese, crumbled

Method

1 Preheat the oven to 175C/350F/Gas4.

2 Heat 2 tsp of the oil in a frying pan. Sauté the leeks for about 5 minutes until they begin to soften. Season, then stir in the tomatoes and capers. Cover and cook for 3 minutes. Transfer to a bowl.

3 In a different bowl, whisk the egg whites with herbes de Provence and thyme. Season with salt and pepper, then add the egg yolks and whisk until the mixture is fluffy.

4 Heat the remaining teaspoon of oil in a frying pan. Pour in the eggs, then the tomato and leek mixture. Sprinkle the goat's cheese over the top.

5 Cook for about 4 minutes, then slide the pan into the oven and bake for 15-20 minutes, until the eggs are cooked.

6 Serve at once, with gluten free toast and salad.

Chefs Note....
Avoid the white part of the leek, which is high FodMap. Only the green parts should be used.

SERVES 8

Salmon Burgers

Low FODMAP Diet

Ingredients

- 415g/15oz tinned pink salmon
- 2 tbsp fresh dill, chopped, + 1 tbsp
- 2 tbsp fresh chives, chopped
- ¼ tsp ground black pepper
- 1 egg, beaten
- Olive oil cooking spray

Method

1. Drain the salmon, then tip it into a bowl and mash it with a fork. Mix in the dill, chives, and pepper, and then the egg to bind it all together.
2. With your hands, form the mixture into 8 burgers.
3. Heat a large frying pan and spray it lightly with olive oil. Fry the salmon burgers for about 4 minutes on each side.
4. Serve in gluten free rolls with salad, or enjoy like fishcakes with chips and vegetables.

Chefs Note....

To get a good hit of calcium as well as protein from this dish, don't remove the bones from the salmon, just mash them up with the rest of the fish.

SERVES 4

Slow Cooker Chicken Rice Soup

Low FODMAP Diet

Ingredients

- 4 medium carrots, peeled & chopped
- 1 courgette, chopped
- 1lb skinless chicken breasts
- 15g/½oz butter
- ½ tsp dried thyme
- 175g/6oz brown rice
- 1lt/4 cups gluten free, low FodMap chicken stock
- 250ml/1 cup water
- 2 tsp olive oil
- 1 small leek, green parts only, sliced
- Juice from 1 lemon
- Salt & pepper
- 1 tbsp Parmesan cheese, grated
- 4 sprigs parsley to garnish

Method

1 Tip the carrots, courgette, courgette, chicken breasts, butter, thyme, and rice into your slow cooker. Pour in the stock and the water. Cover and cook on Low for 8 hours or on High for 4.

2 Remove the chicken breasts to a chopping board and turn the slow cooker up to High if necessary.

3 Heat the oil in a frying pan. Sauté the leek for about 8 minutes, until tender.

4 Shred the chicken with two forks and return it to the slow cooker. Stir in the leeks, then cover and cook for a few minutes until the chicken is heated through.

5 Turn off the slow cooker before you stir in the lemon juice. Season the soup with salt and pepper to taste.

6 Ladle into bowls and garnish with grated Parmesan and fresh parsley.

Chefs Note....

If you don't have a slow cooker, just use an ordinary large pan. Omit the water and cook for 30-45 minutes instead of 4 or 8 hours.

SERVES 6

Butternut Squash Salad

Low FODMAP Diet

Ingredients

- 600g/1lb5oz butternut squash, peeled, deseeded chopped
- 2 tsp olive oil, + 2 tbsp
- 2 tsp sesame seeds
- 1 tbsp fresh lemon juice
- 3 tsp brown sugar
- 2 tsp wholegrain mustard
- 150g/5oz spinach leaves
- 75g/3oz toasted pine nuts
- Salt & pepper

Method

1 Preheat the oven to 220C/430F/Gas7. Line a baking tray with greaseproof paper.

2 Tip the squash into a large bowl. Drizzle with 2 tsp olive oil, and season well with salt and pepper. Toss the squash until evenly coated in the oil. Arrange it on the baking tray in a single layer.

3 Bake in the oven for 25-30 minutes or until golden brown, turning once half way through cooking.

4 Remove the tray from the oven and scatter the sesame seeds evenly over the squash. Return it to oven and bake for 5 more minutes, until the seeds are lightly toasted. Remove from oven and set aside to cool.

5 In a bowl, whisk together the lemon juice, 2 tbsp olive oil, mustard and brown sugar. Season with salt and pepper.

6 Tip the squash into a bowl. Add the spinach and pine nuts and drizzle the dressing over the top. Toss until everything is coated in the dressing.

7 Serve at once.

Chefs Note....

Enjoy this on its own for lunch, or serve as a side dish with dinner.

SERVES 4

Shrimp Salad

Low FODMAP Diet

Ingredients

- 250g/9oz shrimp, peeled and cooked
- 1 tbsp olive oil
- 500g/1lb 2oz brown rice, cooked weight
- 100g/3½oz cucumber, peeled & chopped
- ½ red pepper, deseeded & chopped
- 125g/4oz green beans, finely sliced
- 75g/3oz feta cheese, crumbled
- Salt & pepper
- 2 tbsp extra virgin olive oil
- 2 tbsp red wine vinegar
- 3 tbsp fresh basil, chopped, + more to garnish
- 3 tbsp fresh parsley, chopped, + more to garnish

Method

1 Heat the olive oil in a frying pan, and fry the shrimp for about 3-5 minutes, until cooked.

2 Meanwhile, in a large bowl, mix together the rice, cucumber, red pepper, beans and feta. In a small bowl whisk together the extra virgin olive oil, red wine vinegar, basil and parsley. Drizzle this dressing over the salad and toss to combine.

3 Divide the salad into 4 serving bowls and place the cooked shrimp on top.

4 Garnish with freshly chopped basil and parsley leaves.

Chefs Note....
A treat to take to work, or to serve to friends at a lunch party.

SERVES 4

Butternut Squash and Lemon Risotto

Low FODMAP Diet

Ingredients

- 250g/9oz butternut squash, peeled, deseeded & chopped
- 2 large carrots, peeled & chopped
- 2 tbsp olive oil
- Salt & pepper
- 300g/11oz Arborio rice
- 50g/2oz leek, green parts only, finely chopped
- 1 tbsp garlic infused olive oil
- 1 tbsp olive oil
- 1lt/4 cups gluten free, low FodMap chicken stock
- 2 lemons, to yield 1 tsp lemon zest & 2½ tbsp juice
- 165g/5½oz spinach, finely chopped
- 3 tbsp fresh coriander, chopped
- 50g/2oz Parmesan cheese, grated

Method

1 Preheat the oven to 200C/400F/Gas6.

2 Place the squash and the carrot on a baking tray in a single layer, and drizzle with 1 tbsp olive oil. Season with salt and pepper.

3 Bake in the oven for 20-25 minutes until the vegetables are soft and lightly golden. Stir them up once or twice during cooking.

4 Meanwhile, heat 1 tbsp olive oil and the garlic infused oil together in a large pan, and fry the leek for a couple of minutes. Stir in the rice and cook gently for another minute.

5 Gradually pour in the chicken stock, a little at a time, allowing the rice to absorb it before adding more. Stir frequently.

6 When the rice is cooked and the stock absorbed, stir in the spinach, lemon juice and lemon zest. Season with salt and pepper to taste. Stir in the roasted squash and carrots, the coriander and the Parmesan.

7 Serve and enjoy.

Chefs Note....

If you like, you can make the risotto even creamier by stirring in 2 tbsp Greek yogurt just before serving.

SERVES 4

Spicy Steak Salad

Low FODMAP Diet

Ingredients

- 2 tsp Lebanese spice mix
- 500g/1lb 2oz beef sirloin steaks
- Olive oil cooking spray
- 1 romaine lettuce, roughly chopped
- 2 medium tomatoes, roughly chopped
- 1 cucumber, roughly chopped
- 1 red pepper, deseeded & chopped
- 16 large olives, pitted & halved
- 1 tbsp extra virgin olive oil
- 2 tbsp red wine vinegar
- 1 tsp Dijon mustard

Method

1 Rub the Baharat spices into both sides of the steaks.

2 Heat a frying pan and spray it with olive oil. Place the steaks in the pan and cook for a minute or two on each side, until they're cooked to your preference.

3 Remove them from the pan and set them aside on a plate to rest for a few minutes.

4 Meanwhile, arrange the lettuce, tomatoes, cucumber, pepper and olives on 4 plates.

5 In a small bowl, whisk together the extra virgin olive oil, vinegar and mustard.

6 Slice the steaks thinly and arrange it over the salad on each plate.

7 Drizzle the olive oil dressing over the top, and serve at once.

Chefs Note....
This makes a fabulous lunch or a light dinner.

SERVES 1

Stuffed Red Pepper

Low FODMAP Diet

Ingredients

- Olive oil cooking spray
- 1 red pepper, deseeded & halved
- 50g/2oz cooked leftover chicken, shredded
- 2 tomatoes, chopped
- 2 basil leaves, torn
- Salt & pepper
- 25g/1oz mozzarella cheese, chopped
- 1 tbsp Parmesan cheese, grated
- Chopped parsley to garnish

Method

1 Preheat the oven to 200C/400F/Gas6. Line a baking tray with parchment. Spray the parchment with oil.

2 Place the pepper halves on the baking tray, cut sides upwards. Divide the chicken between the two halves.

3 Mix the tomatoes and basil together in a bowl. Season with salt and pepper. Spoon this mixture over the chicken in the pepper halves.

4 Scatter the mozzarella evenly into the halves, then sprinkle on the Parmesan. Grind on a little more black pepper.

5 Bake the peppers in the oven for about 20 minutes, until the pepper halves are soft.

6 Serve and enjoy.

Chefs Note....

Use a yellow or orange pepper if you prefer.

SERVES 4

Bacon and Brie Frittata

Low FODMAP Diet

Ingredients

- 1 tbsp olive oil
- 8 rashers smoked bacon
- 6 eggs, lightly beaten
- 1 tbsp chives, chopped
- Freshly ground black pepper, to taste
- 100g/3½oz Brie cheese, sliced

Method

1 Preheat the grill.

2 In a small pan, heat half of the olive oil. Fry the bacon until it's crispy. Drain it on kitchen towel.

3 Heat the remaining oil in a frying pan. In a bowl, mix the eggs together with the bacon, chives and black pepper. Pour the egg mixture into the frying pan and cook over a low heat until it begins to set.

4 Lay the Brie on top of the setting egg, then slide the pan under the grill until the egg is set and golden.

5 Remove it from the pan and cut into wedges just before serving.

Chefs Note....

Enjoy with crunchy salad and gluten-free toast.

SERVES 2

Easy Chicken and Cranberry Sandwich

Low FODMAP Diet

Ingredients

- 350g/12oz cooked chicken breasts, shredded
- 3 tbsp mayonnaise
- 1 tbsp cranberry sauce
- Handful rocket
- 4 slices gluten free bread, spread with non-dairy spread.

Method

1 Mix the chicken and mayonnaise together in a bowl.

2 Divide it between two slices of bread. Top with the rocket and some cranberry sauce.

3 Close the sandwiches and enjoy!

Chefs Note....

Use other salad greens instead of rocket if you prefer. Or use leftover turkey instead of chicken and make a delicious Christmas sandwich!

Chicken Wraps

SERVES 4

Low FODMAP Diet

Ingredients

- ½ cucumber, halved & sliced
- 1 small carrot, peeled & grated
- 1 tbsp white wine vinegar
- 2 tbsp vegetable oil
- 8 boneless, skinless chicken thighs, sliced
- 1 tsp freshly grated ginger
- 3 tbsp light brown soft sugar
- 2 tbsp gluten free soy sauce
- 120ml/½ cup water
- 8 small gluten free wraps
- 2 Little Gem lettuces, leaves separated and halved

Method

1 In a small bowl, mix the cucumber, carrot and white wine vinegar. Set aside.

2 Heat 1 tbsp oil in a frying pan, and fry the chicken until it's fully cooked and golden brown. Remove to a plate and set aside.

3 Reduce the heat and warm the rest of the oil in the pan. Fry the ginger for about 2 minutes until it's softened. Add the sugar, soy sauce and water. Bring to the boil and let it cook for 5 minutes or so until it forms into a sauce.

4 Return the chicken to the pan and heat through.

5 Warm the wraps according to the packet instructions. Spread them on 4 plates. Arrange the lettuce on each, then the chicken mixture, and the cucumber and carrot.

Chefs Note....
Make sure you use low FodMap wraps to avoid irritable ingredients.

20

Low FODMAP

DINNERS

Time to try....
the
LOW FODMAP
DIET

SERVES 2

Rocket Pesto Pasta

Low FODMAP Diet

Ingredients

- Handful rocket leaves
- 165g/5½oz baby spinach leaves
- 50ml/¼ cup extra virgin olive oil
- 2 tbsp pine nuts
- 60g/2½oz Parmesan cheese, + extra to garnish
- Pinch sea salt
- 10 rashers bacon, chopped
- 250g/9oz gluten free pasta

Method

1 Place the rocket, spinach, olive oil, pine nuts, and Parmesan in a blender. Add a large pinch of salt and blend until very smooth.

2 Cook the pasta according to the packet instructions. Drain it and tip it into a bowl. Set aside.

3 Using the pan you cooked the pasta in, fry the bacon until crisp, then return the pasta to the pan, too. Pour in the pesto and toss everything together.

4 Serve with an extra sprinkle of parmesan cheese.

Chefs Note....
Use the traditional basil instead of rocket or spinach if you prefer.

SERVES 2

Fish and Chips

Low FODMAP Diet

Ingredients

- 450g/1lb potatoes, peeled & chopped into chips
- 1 tbsp olive oil, + extra for brushing
- 2 haddock fillets, each weighing approx. 150g/5oz
- Salt & pepper
- Juice & zest of 1 lemon, + wedges to garnish
- Handful fresh parsley, chopped
- 1 tbsp capers, chopped
- 2 tbsp Greek yogurt

Method

1. Preheat the oven to 200C/400F/Gas6.
2. Toss the chips in the oil to coat them, then place them on a baking tray in a single layer. Bake them in the oven for about 40 minutes, until crisp and golden brown.
3. Place the fish in a shallow dish, and brush them lightly with oil. Season with salt and pepper. Drizzle half the lemon juice over them, then bake them in the oven for 10 minutes.
4. Scatter about half the parsley and all the lemon zest over the fish, and bake for another 2-5 minutes until they just flake against a fork.
5. Meanwhile, in a bowl, combine the capers, yogurt, the remaining parsley and the lemon juice. Season to taste, and set aside.
6. Serve the chips and fish side by side on plates with a spoonful of the capers and yogurt mix between.

Chefs Note....

Greek yogurt is low FodMap in small amounts like this, but if you can't tolerate it, use lactose free yogurt instead.

SERVES 6

Chicken Casserole

Low FODMAP Diet

Ingredients

- 1 tbsp garlic infused olive oil
- 6 chicken drumsticks
- 6 boneless, skinless chicken thighs
- 1kg/2¼lb small potatoes, halved
- 2 medium tomatoes, finely chopped
- 100g/3½oz olives
- 1 tbsp fresh rosemary leaves
- 120ml/½ cup dry white wine
- Salt & pepper

Method

1 Preheat the oven to 200C/400F/Gas6.

2 Heat the oil in a flameproof baking dish and cook the chicken drumsticks for 5 minutes, turning occasionally, until they're evenly browned.

3 Remove them to a plate and cover to keep them warm. Brown the chicken thighs in the same dish, then transfer them to the warming plate.

4 Tip the potatoes into to the dish and cook, turning occasionally, for about 5 minutes until they're golden.

5 Remove the dish from the heat. Return the chicken to the dish and add the tomato, olives and rosemary. Pour the wine over the top and season with salt and pepper.

6 Bake in the oven for around 45 minutes, until the chicken juices run clear and the potato is tender.

7 Serve and enjoy.

Chefs Note....
1 small glass of wine is allowed on a low FodMap diet.

SERVES 1

Sweet and Sour Beef

Low FODMAP Diet

Ingredients

- 2 tbsp tomato puree
- 1 tbsp maple syrup
- 1 tsp gluten free soy sauce
- 1 tsp rice vinegar
- 1 tbsp sesame oil
- 2 spring onions, green parts only, chopped
- 1 red pepper
- 1 tsp freshly grated ginger
- 75g/3oz sirloin steak, cut into thin strips
- 1 tbsp garlic infused oil
- 1 tbsp sesame seeds

Method

1 In a small pan heat the tomato puree, maple syrup, soy sauce and rice vinegar, stirring well to combine. Once hot, set aside.

2 In a different pan, heat the sesame oil and sauté the spring onion, peppers and ginger for 3 minutes or so until they begin to soften.

3 Add the strips of beef and fry for a further 4 or 5 minutes, or until the beef is cooked to your preference.

4 Pour in the sweet and sour sauce, the garlic infused oil and the sesame seeds. Stir until the beef is evenly coated.

5 Serve at once with brown rice or gluten free noodles.

Chefs Note....

Feel free to adjust the quantities of maple syrup and vinegar to suit your own sweet and sour taste.

Lamb Skewers

SERVES 2

Low FODMAP Diet

Ingredients

- 1 tbsp toasted sesame oil
- 1 tbsp ground cumin
- 1 tsp ground coriander
- 125g/4oz peanut butter
- 120ml/½ cup coconut milk
- 2 tbsp gluten free Tamari sauce
- 1 tsp maple syrup

Method

1 Blend together the coriander, spring onions, the juice of 1 lime and salt. Pour the mixture over the lamb in a shallow dish or container, and stir to coat all the meat. Marinate, covered, for at least 12 hours, preferably 24.

2 Preheat the grill. Prong the lamb pieces on to skewers, and cook them under the grill for 4-6 minutes, turning once to ensure even cooking.

3 Meanwhile, in a small pan heat the juice of the remaining lime, sesame oil, cumin, coriander, peanut butter, coconut milk, Tamari and maple syrup. Stir well to combine.

4 Serve the sauce alongside the lamb skewers.

Chefs Note....

You could also BBQ the skewers on a summer evening.

SERVES 1

Glazed Salmon Fillet

Low FODMAP Diet

Ingredients

- 225g/8oz salmon filet
- 2 tbsp maple syrup
- 1 tbsp garlic infused oil
- 1 tbsp gluten-free soy sauce
- Salt & pepper
- 1 tbsp sesame seeds

Method

1 Preheat the oven to 200C/400F/Gas6.

2 In small bowl whisk together the maple syrup, garlic infused oil, and soy sauce. Season with a little pepper to taste. Pour it over the salmon in a baking dish and turn to coat the fish thoroughly. Leave to marinate in the fridge for half an hour.

3 Sprinkle the marinated salmon with sesame seeds, then bake it in the oven, uncovered, for about 20 minutes, until it flakes against a fork.

4 Serve with low FodMap vegetables and potatoes or brown rice.

Chefs Note....

Enjoy the flavour of garlic through the infused oil, without suffering from the fructans in garlic which are water soluble and don't leak into the oil.

SERVES 4

Beef Stroganoff

Low FODMAP Diet

Ingredients

- 2 tsp olive oil
- 1 tsp garlic-infused olive oil
- 60g/2½oz white cabbage, finely sliced
- 150g/5oz spring onions, green parts only, finely chopped
- 1½ x 425g/15oz can mushrooms in brine, drained, well rinsed & sliced
- 500g/1lb 2oz beef, cut into strips
- 1 tbsp gluten-free, low FodMap flour
- 1 tsp paprika
- 1 gluten free, low FodMap stock cube, crumbled
- 2 tbsp tomato puree
- 2 tsp Dijon mustard
- 250ml/1 cup water
- 2 tbsp coconut yoghurt
- Flat leaf parsley, to garnish

Method

1 Heat the olive oil and the garlic infused oil in a large frying pan. Sauté the cabbage for about 4 minutes, until it softens.

2 Stir in the spring onions and mushrooms, and cook for another 2 minutes. Tip the vegetables into a bowl.

3 Turn up the heat and brown the beef strips in the same pan.

4 Meanwhile, in a bowl, mix together the flour, paprika and crumbled stock cube.

5 Lower the heat under the frying pan again and add the flour mixture to the beef, stirring to coat it. Cook for about 1 minute more, then stir in the tomato puree and mustard. Pour in a little of the water, stirring quickly, then stir in the rest of the water.

6 Return the vegetable mixture to the pan and stir well. Simmer for 3 or 4 minutes while the sauce thickens.

7 Remove the pan from the heat, then stir in the yoghurt and scatter with parsley.

8 Serve with gluten free pasta, potatoes, or rice.

SERVES 4

Beef and Red Wine Stew

Low FODMAP Diet

Ingredients

- 1 tbsp olive oil
- 3 rashers bacon, chopped
- 650g/1lb7oz beef, chopped
- 1 tbsp gluten free flour
- 3 medium carrots, peeled & chopped
- 1 stalk celery, finely sliced
- ½ small swede, chopped
- Handful fresh thyme leaves
- 500ml/2 cups red wine
- Salt & pepper

Method

1 Heat the oil in a large pan and fry the bacon. Coat the beef in the flour and add it to the pan too.

2 Once the meat is browned, tip in the vegetables and thyme. Then pour in the wine and season with salt and pepper.

3 Bring to a simmer and cook for about 2 hours, stirring occasionally.

4 Serve with boiled or mashed potatoes.

Chefs Note....
The alcohol in this recipe should all boil off, but in any case it is a small enough quantity to tolerate.

SERVES 6

Thai Chicken Curry

Low FODMAP Diet

Ingredients

- 2 green chillies, deseeded & roughly chopped
- 2 tbsp freshly grated ginger
- Handful fresh coriander, roughly chopped
- 1 stalk lemon grass, chopped
- 1 lime, zest & juice
- 4 kaffir lime leaves, chopped
- 2 tsp coriander seeds
- 1 tsp ground cumin
- ½ tsp whole black peppercorns
- 2 tsp fish sauce
- 2 tbsp olive oil
- 6 boneless, skinless chicken thighs, sliced
- 2 medium carrots, peeled & chopped
- ½ red pepper, deseeded & chopped
- 400ml/14floz can coconut milk
- 250ml/1 cup gluten free, low FodMap chicken stock
- 2 tsp sugar, to taste
- Sea salt, to taste

Method

1 Using a food processor or a mortar and pestle, grind the chilli, ginger, coriander, lemon grass, lime zest and juice, kaffir lime leaves, coriander seeds, cumin, peppercorns, fish sauce and olive oil into a smooth paste.

2 Heat the olive oil in a large pan and scrape in the paste. Fry for a couple minutes until aromatic.

3 Stir in the chicken, carrots and pepper until thoroughly coated with the curry paste, then pour in the coconut milk and chicken stock and stir well.

4 Lower the heat and simmer for about 45 minutes, until the sauce has thickened.

5 Add sugar and salt to taste, then serve with brown rice.

Chefs Note....

Garnish with freshly chopped coriander leaves and a wedge of lime.

SERVES 2

Roasted Sea Bass

Low FODMAP Diet

Ingredients

- 300g/11oz potatoes, finely sliced
- 1 red pepper, deseeded & cut into strips
- 2 tbsp extra virgin olive oil
- 1 tbsp rosemary leaves, finely chopped
- 2 sea bass fillets
- 25g/1oz olives, pitted & halved
- ½ lemon, finely sliced
- Handful fresh basil leaves, to garnish

Method

1 Preheat the oven to 180C/350F/Gas4.

2 Spread the potato and pepper slices on a large non-stick baking tray. Drizzle them with 1 tbsp olive oil and sprinkle the rosemary over the top. Season with salt and pepper.

3 Mix it all together to coat the vegetables in the oil and herbs, and then roast in the oven for 25 mins, turning once during cooking, until the potatoes are golden and crisp at the edges.

4 Place the fish fillets on top of the roasted vegetables, and scatter on the olives.

5 Arrange the lemon slices over the fish and sprinkle on the rest of the olive oil.

6 Return the tray to the oven and roast for around another 8 minutes, until the fish is cooked and flakes against a fork.

7 Serve garnished with fresh basil leaves.

Chefs Note....

Sea bass is an important source of protein and omega 3 which are both important ingredients in a low FodMap diet.

SERVES 4

Fish in Lemon Oatmeal Dressing

Low FODMAP Diet

Ingredients

- 75g/3oz oatmeal
- 2 tbsp parsley, chopped
- 2 tbsp finely grated lemon zest
- 75g/3oz gluten free flour
- 2 eggs, lightly beaten
- 4 firm white fish fillets, each weighing approx. 175g/6oz
- 2 cucumbers
- 1 carrot, peeled & chopped into julienne sticks
- 60g/2½oz bean sprouts
- 4 tbsp vegetable oil
- 125g/4oz salad leaf mix

Method

1 On a large plate, mix together the oatmeal, parsley and lemon rind. Tip the flour onto a separate plate and season it with salt and pepper. Place the egg in a shallow bowl.

2 Coat the fish in the flour, then dip it in the egg, then in the oat mixture, pressing firmly to coat it thoroughly. Place the coated fish on a clean plate and chill it in the fridge for half an hour.

3 Meanwhile, with a potato peeler, slice the cucumbers lengthways into thin strips. Combine the cucumber strips, carrot and bean sprouts in a large bowl.

4 Heat the oil in a large frying pan and fry 2 fish at a time, about 4 or 5 minutes on each side, or until the flesh flakes against a fork.

5 Serve the fish with the mixed salad leaves and the cucumber mixture.

Chefs Note....

Try using Lebanese cucumbers if you can source them.

SERVES 4

Chicken in Creamy Pesto Sauce

Low FODMAP Diet

Ingredients

- 1 tbsp olive oil
- 4 boneless skinless chicken breasts
- 200g/7oz tomatoes, halved
- 1 tbsp tomato puree
- 3 tbsp low FodMap pesto
- 3 tbsp lactose free double cream
- Fresh basil leaves, torn

Method

1 Heat the oil in a frying pan, and fry the chicken breast, turning occasionally, for 15 minutes or so, until the chicken is cooked and the juices run clear. Season it all over with a little salt and pepper.

2 Add the tomato halves to the pan, and cook until they start to soften. Lower the heat and stir in the tomato puree, pesto and lactose free cream. Continue to cook for a few more minutes, stirring until you have a sauce.

3 Scatter with some basil, and serve with brown rice and salad.

Chefs Note....

You can make your own low FodMap pesto with garlic infused olive oil, basil, pine nuts and some Parmesan cheese.

Pulled Pork

SERVES 12

Low FODMAP Diet

Ingredients

- 1 tbsp olive oil
- 2 tbsp honey
- Salt & pepper
- 1 rolled pork joint, weighing approx. 1.35kg/3lbs
- 225g/8oz passata/sieved tomatoes
- 1 tbsp Worcestershire sauce
- 1 tbsp dark brown soft sugar
- 1 tsp mustard
- 1 tsp vinegar

Method

1 In a bowl, mix together the olive oil, honey, salt and pepper.

2 Place the pork on a large sheet of foil, and rub in the oil and honey mixture. Wrap it in the foil, place it on a baking dish and roast in the oven for an hour, or until the pork is very tender.

3 Meanwhile, in a pan, mix together the tomato ketchup, Worcestershire sauce, brown sugar, mustard, and vinegar. Cook for around 15 minutes, stirring occasionally, until the sauce thickens.

4 Place the pork on a chopping board, leave it to cool for a few minutes, and then shred it with two forks. Stir the meat into the sauce.

5 Serve with vegetables and spicy potato wedges or in sandwiches made from gluten free bread or rolls.

Chefs Note....

Check the passata ingredients to make sure there is no added onion or garlic.

SERVES 4

Spaghetti Bolognese

Low FODMAP Diet

Ingredients

- 2 tbsp olive oil
- 500g/1lb2oz lean steak mince
- 400g/14oz can chopped tomatoes
- 3 tbsp tomato puree
- 40g/1½oz leek, green parts only, finely chopped
- 125g/4oz baby spinach, chopped
- 1 tsp dried oregano
- 1 tsp dried basil
- ½ tsp dried thyme
- Salt & pepper
- 300g/11oz gluten free spaghetti
- 60g/2½oz Parmesan cheese

Method

1 Heat 1 tbsp olive oil in a large frying pan and brown the mince. Stir in the tomatoes, tomato puree, leek, spinach and herbs.

2 Simmer for about 20 minutes, stirring occasionally. Season with salt and pepper.

3 Cook the spaghetti according to the instructions on the packet. Drain and toss with the remaining olive oil.

4 Serve the sauce on top of the spaghetti and sprinkle with a little Parmesan.

Chefs Note....

Parmesan is a low FodMap cheese and allowed in small quantities.

SERVES 2

Salmon with Spinach and Cream Sauce

Low FODMAP Diet

Ingredients

- 1 tsp olive oil
- 2 large boneless salmon fillets
- Salt & pepper
- 250g/9oz spinach
- 2 tbsp crème fraîche
- 1 lemon, ½ juiced, ½ cut into wedges
- 1 tsp capers, drained
- 2 tbsp parsley, chopped

Method

1 Heat the oil in a pan and season the salmon on both sides.

2 Place the salmon in the pan, skin side down then fry for about 4-5 minutes, depending on the thickness of your fillet, until the colour changes most of the way up the fish.

3 Turn the fillets and fry the other side for a couple of minutes, until the flesh flakes against a fork.

4 Remove the fish to a plate to rest, and set aside.

5 Place the spinach in the same hot pan. Season well with salt and a little pepper, then cover and leave to wilt for 1 minute, stirring it up occasionally.

6 Divide the spinach between two plates, and arrange the salmon on top.

7 Pour the crème fraîche into the same pan. Stir in the lemon juice, capers and parsley, and season to taste. Heat gently, being careful not to boil. Spoon the sauce over the fish, and serve garnished with lemon wedges.

Chefs Note....

Small quantities of crème fraiche is allowed on the low FodMap diet, but you can also use Greek or lactose- free yogurt instead.

SERVES 6

Greek Roasted Lamb

Low FODMAP Diet

Ingredients

- 75g/3oz feta cheese, crumbled
- 3 tbsp fresh mint, chopped, + a few extra leaves to garnish
- 50g/2oz olives, pitted & chopped
- 2 tsp lemon zest
- 1 tbsp pine nuts
- 900g/2lb lamb roast
- 2 tsp olive oil
- Balsamic vinegar, to garnish
- Mint leaves, extra, to garnish

Method

1 In a bowl, mix together the feta, mint, olives, lemon zest and pine nuts. Cut about 6 deep pockets around the lamb (without cutting all the way through) and pack each pocket with the feta stuffing. Secure the pockets with cocktail sticks.

2 Brush the lamb all over with the olive oil. Heat a large frying pan over high heat. Brown the lamb for a minute or two on each side, then place it on a baking tray.

3 Roast it in the oven for about 40 minutes or until the lamb is done to your preference.

4 Remove from the oven, cover loosely with foil and leave to rest for at least 10 minutes.

5 Remove the cocktail sticks and slice. Serve garnished with the extra mint leaves and a drizzle of balsamic vinegar if you wish.

Chefs Note....

Enjoy with boiled potatoes and low FodMap vegetables.

SERVES 4

Creamy Tomato Gnocchi

Low FODMAP Diet

Ingredients

- 1 tbsp olive oil
- 400g/14oz tinned chopped tomatoes
- Salt & pepper
- 140g/4½oz lactose free double cream
- 1 tbsp garlic infused oil
- 500g/1lb2oz gluten free gnocchi
- 200g/7oz baby spinach
- Basil leaves, to garnish
- Grated Parmesan cheese, to garnish

Method

1 Heat the olive oil in a frying pan. Add the tomatoes, season them with salt and pepper and cook them gently for about 10 minutes.

2 Stir in the cream and the garlic infused oil, and cook for a couple of minutes longer.

3 Meanwhile, in a large pan, boil the gnocchi according to the packet directions. Add the spinach for the final minute of cooking. Drain, return to the pan, then pour on the sauce and mix it through.

4 Serve at once, garnished with basil leaves and a little grated Parmesan if you wish.

Chefs Note....
You can buy packets of gluten free gnocchi, or make your own.

SERVES 4

Meatloaf with Tomato Sauce

Low FODMAP Diet

Ingredients

- 500g/1lb2oz steak mince
- 2 tbsp parsley finely chopped
- 1 egg, beaten
- 75g/3oz gluten free breadcrumbs
- 100g/3½oz tomato puree
- 1 tbsp lactose free yoghurt
- Salt & pepper
- 400g/14oz can tomatoes
- Pinch of dried thyme

Method

1 Preheat the oven to 200C/400F/Gas6.

2 In a bowl mix together the mince, parsley, egg, breadcrumbs, tomato puree, and yoghurt. Season well with salt and pepper.

3 Turn the mixture out onto a baking tray and with your (clean!) hands, shape it into a loaf. Set aside.

4 In a clean bowl, mix together the tomatoes and thyme and season to taste. Pour the mixture around the loaf in the baking tray. Bake together in the oven for 25-30 minutes.

5 When it's baked, slice the meatloaf and serve it with the tomato sauce.

Chefs Note....

Enjoy with mashed potatoes (mash them with non-dairy spread and almond milk) and low Fodmap vegetables such as carrot and kale.

SERVES 2

Nutty Tofu

Low FODMAP Diet

Ingredients

- 2 tbsp gluten free soy sauce
- 2 tsp toasted sesame oil
- 225g/8oz extra firm tofu, cubed
- 3 tbsp sesame seeds
- 1 tbsp peanut oil
- 100g/3½oz broccoli, roughly chopped
- 2 tsp garlic infused oil
- 1 tsp freshly grated ginger
- 25g/1oz walnuts

Method

1 In a bowl, mix together the soy sauce and sesame oil. Tip in the tofu and toss together to coat. Leave to marinate in the fridge for at least 15 minutes, preferably 2 hours.

2 Drain the tofu, then sprinkle it with the sesame seeds.

3 Heat the peanut oil in a frying pan. Add the tofu, broccoli, garlic-infused oil and ginger. Cook for about 2 minutes, stir gently and then cook for another 5 minutes until the broccoli is tender. Stir in the nuts.

4 Serve and enjoy!

Chefs Note....

Tofu is low in FodMaps and high in protein, calcium and iron, so is a useful ingredient in a low FodMap diet.

SERVES 4

Green Lamb Curry

Low FODMAP Diet

Ingredients

- 2 tbsp garlic infused olive oil
- 2 tsp freshly grated ginger
- 1 red chilli, deseeded & finely chopped
- 2 tsp ground cumin
- 2 tsp ground coriander
- 1 tsp turmeric
- 600g/1lb5oz lamb, diced
- 300g/11oz fresh tomatoes, blended
- 200g/7oz spinach
- 5 spring onions, green parts only, roughly chopped
- Handful fresh coriander leaves
- Salt & pepper

Method

1 Heat the oil in a pan and sauté the ginger and most of the chilli for a few seconds. Add the cumin, coriander, and turmeric and cook for a minute more. Mix in the lamb, coating it in the spices. Brown it on all sides then stir in the blended tomatoes.

2 Reduce the heat, cover and simmer for an hour, stirring occasionally, until the lamb is tender.

3 Blend together the spinach, spring onion and most of the coriander until it forms a smooth paste. Stir this mixture into the curry and cook for 5 minutes. Adjust the seasoning.

4 Serve over steamed brown rice, garnished with the remaining coriander leaves and a little chopped red chilli.

Chefs Note....
If you have leftovers, you can freeze them for another day.

15

Low FODMAP

DESSERTS

Time to try....

the LOW FODMAP DIET

SERVES 6

Kiwi Fruit Sponge

Low FODMAP Diet

Ingredients

- 2 large eggs
- 60g/2½oz caster sugar
- 60g/2½oz gluten free plain flour
- 120ml/¼ cup lactose free double cream
- 3 kiwi fruit, peeled & sliced

Method

1 Preheat the oven to 200C/400F/Gas6. Grease a 20cm round cake tin, then line the base with parchment.

2 In a large bowl, whisk together the eggs and caster sugar until pale and very thick. Sift in the flour and gently fold it in.

3 Tip the mixture into the cake tin and bake in the oven for about 15 minutes until it's golden brown and a skewer comes out of it clean.

4 Turn the cake out onto a wire rack to cool.

5 When it's completely cool, whisk the cream in a bowl until it thickens, then spread it over the cake. Arrange the kiwi slices on top.

Chefs Note....

If you can't get lactose free cream, try draining Greek yogurt in a sieve in the fridge overnight – it makes the yogurt much creamier.

SERVES 8

Blueberry Crumble

Low FODMAP Diet

Ingredients

- 150g/5oz sugar, + 50g/2oz
- 350g/12oz gluten free self-raising flour
- ¼ tsp salt
- ½ tsp ground cinnamon
- 250g/9oz olive oil spread, softened
- 1 large egg, lightly beaten
- 400g/14oz fresh or frozen blueberries
- 3 tsp gluten free cornflour

Method

1. Preheat the oven to 180C/350F/Gas4. Grease a 20 x 30cm baking tin.
2. In a bowl, mix together the sugar, flour, salt and cinnamon. Add the egg and the olive spread and blend everything together with a fork. Rub the mixture between your fingers to form large moist crumbs.
3. Turn half of the mixture into the baking tin and press it down into the base to make an even layer. Tip the blueberries over the top.
4. In a small bowl mix together the remaining sugar and the cornflour. Sprinkle this over the blueberries.
5. Spread the remaining dough over the top.
6. Bake in the oven for 30 minutes, until the top is golden.
7. Allow to cool, then slice into 15.

Chefs Note....

Delicious with low FodMap ice cream, but only eat 1 piece per sitting.

SERVES 6

Strawberry Cheesecake

Low FODMAP Diet

Ingredients

- 200g/7oz rice cakes
- 25g/1oz dark chocolate
- 75g/3oz olive oil spread, melted
- 600g/1lb5oz silken tofu
- 250g/9oz lactose free natural yoghurt
- 60g/2½oz maple syrup
- 2 tsp vanilla essence
- 1 tbsp lemon juice
- 5 tsp gelatine, dissolved in 3 tbsp warm water
- 250g/9oz strawberries, hulled, + a few extra to garnish

Method

1. In your food processor, blend the rice cookies and chocolate to fine crumbs. Add the melted olive spread, and blend again to combine.

2. Line the bottom of a springform cake tin with greaseproof paper and then press the biscuit mixture down into the base to form an even layer. Chill in the fridge to set.

3. Wash your food processor bowl, then blend the silken tofu until very smooth. Pour in the natural yoghurt, maple syrup and lemon juice, and blend again. Add in the dissolved gelatine and blend again. Pour out half the mixture into a separate bowl.

4. Add the strawberries to the mixture still in your food processor, and blend them in until smooth.

5. Take the chilled base from the fridge and pour in the plain tofu mixture Pour the strawberry tofu mixture on top of that. Using a thin knife or a skewer, swirl the mixture without touching the base.

6. Put the cheesecake back in the fridge and leave to set for at least 6 hours.

7. Once set, release the cake tin spring and use a warm knife to slice it. Serve with the extra strawberries.

Raspberry Crunch

SERVES 4

Low FODMAP Diet

Ingredients

- 250g/9oz raspberries
- 2 tbsp orange liqueur
- Zest and juice of 1 orange
- 100g/3½oz dark chocolate
- 3 tbsp almond milk
- 50g/2oz caster sugar
- 6 tbsp gluten free, low FodMap muesli

Method

1 Divide the raspberries between 4 dessert glasses. Sprinkle a little Cointreau and orange zest and juice over each. Set aside.

2 Pour the soy milk into a bowl. Melt the chocolate in the microwave, or in a bowl over a pan of boiling water, and stir it into the milk. Set aside.

3 Tip the sugar into a pan along with 3 tbsp water. Cook gently, without stirring, for 6 or 7 minutes, until the sugar melts and starts to turn golden brown. Stir in the muesli, then pour the mixture onto a baking tray lined with parchment. Leave to cool, then break into thin shards.

4 Divide the chocolate mixture between the glasses and allow to cool, but don't refrigerate. Scatter the crunchy muesli mixture over the top, and serve.

Chefs Note....

Almond milk is lovely with desserts, but feel free to use whichever non-dairy milk you prefer.

Raspberry Ripple Ice Cream

Low FODMAP Diet

Ingredients

- 400ml/14floz can coconut milk
- 125g/4oz fresh raspberries
- 2 tsp liquid glucose, + 120ml/½ cup
- 40g/1½oz coconut sugar
- 1 tsp vanilla extract
- 4 egg whites

Method

1 Keep the coconut milk tin in the fridge overnight. In a pan, mix together the raspberries, glucose, 2 tsp of the coconut sugar and half the vanilla. Cook, stirring occasionally, for about 6 minutes, until the sugar dissolves. Tip the raspberries into a bowl to cool for 30 minutes, then transfer them to the fridge.

2 Spoon off the solidified cream from the top of the can of coconut milk and put it in a measuring jug until you have 220ml. Whisk the coconut cream until it thickens.In a separate bowl, whisk the egg whites into firm peaks.

3 Put the remaining coconut sugar into a pan with the remaining glucose and the vanilla. Cook gently, stirring constantly, for 2 minutes or until the sugar is almost all dissolved. Bring to a simmer, then cook without stirring, for another couple of minutes.

4 Whisking constantly, slowly add this syrup to the egg whites. Whisk for another 4 minutes or so until the mixture is very thick. Leave to cool for a couple of minutes, then gently fold in the coconut cream.

5 Pour half the combined mixture into a loaf tin. Spoon about 2/3 of the raspberry syrup onto the coconut mixture. Use a knife to swirl them together to create a ripple effect. Pour the remaining coconut mixture on top, then the remaining raspberry mixture. Ripple those too. Place n the freezer for 8 hours or until the ice cream is firm.

6 Remove from the freezer 10 mins before serving.

SERVES 8

Summer Fruit Pudding

Low FODMAP Diet

Ingredients

- 750g/1lb11oz mixed summer berries
- 1 medium gluten free white loaf, thinly sliced, crusts removed
- 2 tbsp raspberry liqueur
- 175g/6oz caster sugar

Method

1 Stir the fruit and the sugar together in a pan and bring gently to the boil.

2 When the juices begin to flow, increase the heat and simmer for about 2-3 minutes. Remove from the heat and stir in the raspberry liqueur.

3 With a pastry cutter, cut a circle out of one slice of bread to fit the bottom of a serving bowl, then cut the remaining slices into triangular wedges.

4 Dip one side of the bread circle into the cooked fruit, then place the circle in the bottom of the bowl, juice-side down. Dip the bread triangles in the same way, and arrange them around the edge of the bowl like a lining.

5 Once the bowl is completely lined, tip all the fruit and juices from the pan into the bowl. Cover with more bread wedges. Then place a plate or saucer onto the bread and weigh it down with something heavy.

6 Once the bowl cools enough, chill it in the fridge overnight.

7 When you're ready to serve it, remove the weight and plate. Run a knife around the edges of the pudding then turn the bowl upside down onto a large serving plate. Turn the pudding out, and cut in slices.

SERVES 2

Fun Chocolate Bananas

Low FODMAP Diet

Ingredients

- 3 medium un-ripened bananas,
- 40g/1½oz dark dairy-free chocolate, cut into small pieces
- 25ml/1floz almond milk

Method

1 Pour the almond milk into a microwaveable bowl, add the chocolate and heat in the microwave for 30 second blasts, stirring between each, until the chocolate has all melted and blended into the milk. Alternatively melt it over a pan of boiling water.

2 Cut each banana in two. Dip the flat end of each banana into the melted chocolate and then dip a knife or chopstick in the chocolate to make patterns or pictures (e.g. faces) on the bananas.

3 Stand the banana halves on a non-stick tray and chill them in the fridge for at least 15 minutes to harden off the chocolate.

4 Use a knife to remove the bananas from the tray and serve.

Chefs Note....
Children will love decorating – and eating! – these!

SERVES 6

Banana and Melon Sorbet

Low FODMAP Diet

Ingredients

- 3 chopped frozen un-ripened bananas
- 350g/12oz chopped frozen Cantaloupe melon
- 2 tbsp fresh mint leaves, finely chopped
- 120ml/½ cup almond milk

Method

1 Blend the frozen banana, melon and mint together until crumbly.

2 Pour in the milk a little at a time, whizzing after each addition, until the sorbet becomes smooth.

3 Serve immediately or store in the freezer until you want it.

Chefs Note....

It's always best to use firm/unripe bananas as they contain more fructans once they begin to turn brown.

MAKES 20 TRUFFLES

Chocolate Hazelnut Truffles

Low FODMAP Diet

Ingredients

- 100g/3½oz roasted hazelnuts, + extra, chopped, to garnish
- 100g/3½oz walnuts
- 3 tbsp cocoa powder
- ½ tsp sea salt
- 2 tbsp maple syrup
- 1 tsp pure vanilla extract
- 2 tbsp coconut oil, melted

Method

1 Set aside 20 whole hazelnuts for the centres of the truffles.

2 Tip the rest of the hazelnuts and the walnuts into your blender or food processor and whizz them into small pieces.

3 Add the cocoa and sea salt and blend again. Pour in the maple syrup, vanilla extract and coconut oil and blend until the ingredients start to stick together. Scrape down the sides of the blender as necessary.

4 Roll the mixture into small balls and push a whole hazelnut into the centre of each.

5 Roll them in the chopped hazelnuts to cover.

6 Place the truffle balls in the freezer for half an hour to harden, then store in the fridge until you're ready to eat.

Chefs Note....

To keep within the FodMap limit, you shouldn't eat more than 2 of these truffles in one sitting.

SERVES 2

Orange and Chocolate Pudding

Low FODMAP Diet

Ingredients

- 250ml/1 cup almond milk
- 1 tbsp chia seeds
- 3 tbsp cocoa powder
- 1 tsp vanilla extract
- 1 tbsp freshly squeezed orange juice
- 1 tsp orange zest
- 1 tbsp maple syrup
- 2 orange slices, to garnish

Method

1 Whisk all the ingredients together in a bowl until thoroughly combined.

2 Cover and chill in the fridge for at least an hour, or preferably overnight.

3 Top with orange slices and serve.

Chefs Note....
The addition of chia seeds provides a boost of protein, fibre and omega 3.

SERVES 4

Rice Pudding

Low FODMAP Diet

Ingredients

- 1lt/4 cups light coconut milk, + 1 tbsp
- 110g/3½oz Arborio rice
- 2 tbsp caster sugar
- ½ tsp vanilla extract
- 1 tsp cornflour
- 4 tbsp strawberry jam, warmed

Method

1 Heat the milk and rice in a pan, stirring constantly, until it almost boils. Turn the heat right down and gently cook, stirring occasionally, for 30-40 minutes until the rice is tender.

2 Stir in the sugar and vanilla extract to the rice. Continue stirring until the sugar all dissolves.

3 In a small bowl, whisk the cornflour with 1 tbsp milk to make a smooth paste. Pour it into the rice, stirring constantly. Cook for another couple of minutes until the pudding thickens.

4 Divide the rice pudding between 4 bowls, and serve immediately, each drizzled with 1 tablespoon of warm strawberry jam.

Chefs Note....

Feel free to use any low FodMap milk instead of coconut. Try also sprinkling with cinnamon instead of jam.

SERVES 4

Melon Balls with Lime and Mint Yogurt

Low FODMAP Diet

Ingredients

- ½ honeydew melon
- ½ Cantaloupe melon
- 300g/11oz plain lactose-free, low FodMap yogurt
- 2 tbsp fresh mint leaves, finely chopped, + extra to garnish
- Zest of 1 lime

Method

1 In a bowl, mix together the yogurt, chopped mint and lime zest. Mix it a couple of hours before serving if possible, to let the flavours infuse.

2 Use a melon baller to make small balls from the melons. Put a mix of honeydew and Cantaloupe in each of 4 serving glasses or dishes, no more than 11 or 12 balls in each dish.

3 Add a good dollop of the lime and mint yogurt to each serving, and garnish with a few extra mint leaves.

4 Enjoy!

Chefs Note....

Both types of melon are low FodMap fruits, providing you don't exceed 90g, so don't eat more than 1 serving at a time.

Chocolate Cake

SERVES 6

Low FODMAP Diet

Ingredients

- 1 can pitted prunes in fruit juice
- 150g/5oz gluten free flour
- 50g/2oz cocoa powder
- 1½ tsp baking powder
- 1 tsp bicarbonate of soda
- 100g/3½oz caster sugar
- 3 tbsp vegetable oil
- 250ml/1 cup almond milk
- ½ tsp vanilla extract

Method

1 Preheat the oven to 180C/350F/Gas4. Grease two 19 cm cake tins.

2 Empty the can of pitted prunes, with about half the juice, into a blender and puree. Put 75g/3oz of the puree into a bowl and set aside.

3 Sift the flour, cocoa, baking powder, bicarbonate of soda and sugar into a bowl and mix. Stir in the vegetable oil, almond milk, vanilla extract and the prune puree you've set aside. Mix it all into a smooth batter.

4 Divide the batter evenly between the two cake tins, and bake them both in the oven for about 15 minutes, until a skewer comes out clean.

5 Allow the cakes to cool for 5 minutes or so, before removing them from the tins to a cooling rack.

6 When they're completely cool, ice one cake with your favourite butter or chocolate icing. Spread the other with jam or dairy-free chocolate spread, and place the iced cake on top.

7 Slice and enjoy!

Chefs Note....

With wheat-free cakes, it's best to freeze for later any that won't be eaten the same day.

SERVES 4

Coconut & Chocolate Sorbet with Strawberries

Low FODMAP Diet

Ingredients

- 2 frozen unripened bananas, chopped into chunks
- 1 tbsp cocoa
- 60ml/¼ cup almond milk
- 1 tbsp desiccated coconut, + extra to garnish
- 200g/7oz strawberries, hulled & sliced

Method

1 In your blender or food processor, blend the bananas until they're crumbly.

2 Add the cocoa and milk and blend again until nearly smooth. Add the coconut, scrape down the sides of the bowl or blender, and blend once more.

3 Eat immediately, if you prefer a soft consistency, or if you like your sorbet firmer, tip it into a container and freeze for at least an hour.

4 Divide the strawberries between 4 bowls or glasses, and top with the sorbet. Sprinkle with a little more desiccated coconut, and serve.

Chefs Note....

Don't use ripe bananas as they contain more fructans and become high FodMap.

SERVES 6

Sticky Toffee Pudding

Low FODMAP Diet

Ingredients

- Olive oil cooking spray
- 1 tsp cornflour for dusting
- 75g/3oz non-dairy spread, + 50g/2oz
- 75g/3oz brown sugar, + 100g/3½oz
- 1 egg
- 1 tbsp black treacle
- 75g/3oz gluten free self-raising flour
- 1 tsp bicarbonate of soda
- 200ml/7floz lactose free double cream
- 1 drop vanilla essence
- Pinch salt

Method

1 Preheat the oven to 200C/400F/Gas6. Lightly spray a 1lt oven proof pudding dish with non-stick oil and dust it with cornflour.

2 In a bowl, whisk together 75g/3oz non-dairy spread and 75g/3oz brown sugar. Beat in the egg, the treacle, and the flour. Then mix in the bicarbonate of soda.

3 Turn the mixture out into the oven dish, and bake in the oven for about 25 minutes.

4 Meanwhile melt the rest of the non-dairy spread in a saucepan, then stir in 100g/3½oz brown sugar, the lactose free cream, vanilla essence and salt. When the sugar is melted, simmer for a minute or so until it thickens into a sauce. Pour it into a jug.

5 Divide the pudding between 6 dishes and serve with the sauce.

Chefs Note....

An indulgent yet low FodMap pudding - sure to be a family favourite!

8

Low FODMAP

SMOOTHIES & SNACKS

SERVES 1

Strawberry Smoothie

Low FODMAP Diet

Ingredients

- ½ un-ripened banana, roughly chopped
- 6 medium strawberries, hulled & halved
- 175ml/6floz almond milk
- 1 tsp maple syrup

Method

1. Tip the banana and strawberries into your blender.
2. Pour in the almond milk and the maple syrup.
3. Blend until smooth.
4. Pour into a glass and serve at once.

Chefs Note....

Equally delicious with raspberries or blueberries instead of strawberries. Feel free to use any low FodMap milk instead of almond.

Spiced Nuts

SERVES 4

Low FODMAP Diet

Ingredients

- 150g/5oz walnut halves
- 150g/5oz almonds
- 75g/3oz sunflower seeds
- 3 tbsp maple syrup
- 2 tbsp sesame seeds
- 2 tsp ground cinnamon
- 1 tsp vanilla essence

Method

1 Preheat the oven to 180C/350F/Gas4. Line a baking tray with greaseproof paper.

2 In a large bowl, mix the walnuts, almonds and sunflower seeds. Warm the maple syrup then stir it in with the nuts. Stir in the sesame seeds, cinnamon and vanilla essence.

3 Spread the nut mix out on the baking tray and bake in the oven for 15-20 minutes, until the nuts begin to brown.

4 Remove them from the oven and allow them to cool completely before breaking them up into smaller clumps. Store in an airtight container until needed.

Chefs Note....

This is a super tasty snack which is great to make in advance, store and enjoy later.

SERVES 1

Banana and Cinnamon Smoothie

Low FODMAP Diet

Ingredients

- ½ un-ripened banana, roughly sliced
- 250ml/1 cup soy milk
- 1 tsp cinnamon
- 1 tbsp maple syrup
- Ice

Method

1 Place all the ingredients in your blender.

2 Add a few ice cubes if you wish, and blend until smooth.

3 Pour into a glass and enjoy at once.

Chefs Note....
If you prefer your smoothie less sweet, omit the maple syrup.

SERVES 1

Blueberry Protein Smoothie

Low FODMAP Diet

Ingredients

- 120ml/½ cup almond milk
- 20 blueberries, fresh or frozen
- 60ml/¼ cup vanilla soy ice cream
- 6 ice cubes
- 1/3 frozen un-ripened banana, chopped
- 2 tsp rice protein powder
- 1 tsp chia seeds
- ½ tbsp pure maple syrup
- 1 tsp lemon juice

Method

1. Place all the ingredients into your blender
2. Blend until smooth.
3. Pour the smoothie into a tall glass and serve right away.

Chefs Note....

Rice protein powder is a 'safe' protein to use to supplement your diet.

SERVES 2

Spiced Pineapple and Kale Smoothie

Low FODMAP Diet

Ingredients

- 250ml/1 cup coconut milk
- ½ fresh orange, peeled & broken into segments
- 150g/5oz fresh pineapple, peeled & cut into chunks
- 60g/2½oz kale
- ½ tsp ground ginger
- A few ice cubes

Method

1. Place all the ingredients in your blender.
2. Blend until smooth.
3. Divide the smoothie between 2 glasses, and serve immediately.

Chefs Note....

Use fresh ginger if you wish, and change the amount to suit your own taste.

SERVES 1

Green Smoothie

Low FODMAP Diet

Ingredients

- 50g/2oz baby spinach
- 250ml/1 cup almond milk
- ½ un-ripened frozen banana, chopped
- 1 tbsp peanut butter

Method

1 Drop the spinach into your blender and pour in the almond milk.

2 Blend until the spinach is almost completely broken down.

3 Add the banana and peanut butter and blend again until smooth.

4 Pour into a glass and serve immediately.

Chefs Note....
Most almond milks are fortified with calcium.

SERVES 2

Paprika Popcorn

Low FODMAP Diet

Ingredients

- 50g/2oz unpopped corn
- 2 tbsp vegetable oil
- 1 tbsp golden syrup
- 1 tsp smoked paprika
- Pinch of salt

Method

1 Place the corn in a pan with 1 tbsp of the oil. Cover and heat.

2 Once most of the corn has popped, and the pops have decreased to about 3 seconds apart, remove the pan from the heat.

3 Meanwhile mix the rest of the oil with the maple syrup, paprika and salt to make a paste.

4 Drizzle the paste over the warm popcorn and stir until all the corn is evenly coated.

5 Tip it all into a bowl and serve.

Chefs Note....

Use maple syrup if you prefer. Both maple and golden are low FodMap.

SERVES 4

Guacamole Dip

Low FODMAP Diet

Ingredients

- ½ avocado
- 2 tomatoes, finely diced
- Juice of 1 lime
- Salt & Pepper
- 1 tsp almonds, ground
- 1 tsp pumpkin seeds, ground
- Gluten free corn chips

Method

1 Scoop out the flesh of the avocado and mash it in a bowl. Stir in the tomatoes and lime juice and season to taste with salt and pepper.

2 When you're ready to serve, sprinkle the ground nuts and pumpkin seeds over the top.

3 Serve with gluten free tortilla chips.

Chefs Note....

You can buy gluten free tortilla chips ready-made. Avocados are high in FodMaps but the quantities in a shared dip should be safe for all but the most sensitive.

Other CookNation titles

If you enjoyed 'Time to try... the LOW FODMAP DIET' you may also enjoy other books from CookNation including:

'Time to try... VEGAN'

'Time to try.. .the BLOOD SUGAR DIET"

Time To Try... THE FAST DIET

and the extensive calorie counted '*Skinny*' range of books.

To browse the full catalogue visit
www.bellmackenzie.com

Printed in Great Britain
by Amazon

62362835R00059